If a man does his best, what else is there?

GEORGE S. PATTON

To _Eric_

From _Just some thoughts for a son we love and admire_

Love Mom & Dad

Also by Barbara Milo Ohrbach

The Scented Room

The Scented Room Gardening Notebook

Antiques at Home

Simply Flowers

A Token of Friendship

Memories of Childhood

A Bouquet of Flowers

A Cheerful Heart

The Spirit of America

Merry Christmas

Happy Birthday

All Things Are Possible—Pass the Word

Food for the Soul

Tabletops

If You Think You Can . . . You Can!

Roses for the Scented Room

A Token of Love

Love Your Life

BARBARA MILO OHRBACH

You're the Best

witty words and wisdom
for the greatest guy

CLARKSON POTTER/PUBLISHERS
NEW YORK

Copyright © 2003 by Barbara Milo Ohrbach

Published by Clarkson Potter/Publishers, New York, New York.
Member of the Crown Publishing Group, a division of Random House, Inc.
www.randomhouse.com

CLARKSON N. POTTER is a trademark and POTTER and colophon are registered trademarks of Random House, Inc.

Printed in China

Design by Jan Derevjanik

Library of Congress Cataloging–in–Publication Data is available upon request.

ISBN 0-609-61031-7

10   9   8   7   6   5   4   3   2   1

First Edition

To all my great guys,
especially my husband, Mel

One cannot always be a hero,
but one can always be a man.

GOETHE

Great guys—these words create many different
pictures in our minds. For example, there are the
dedicated, brave men who serve our country in
the military; policemen and firemen who every
day perform selfless deeds; sports legends who
inspire their teams to victory; statesmen who
rise to greatness when they are called upon—
men from all walks of life who make a difference
in so very many ways.

But, for most of us, the greatest guys are our
fathers, husbands, brothers, sons, nephews, uncles,

and friends who provide so much each and every day. The support, courage, guidance, inspiration, strength, humor, love, friendship, gentleness, and warmth they share with us should be treasured. These "ordinary" men are always there, ready and willing to take on whatever the situation calls for. In doing so, they make our lives anything *but* ordinary. They are the ones setting an example for everyone else, even if no one is watching but the dog—aptly proving the maxim that "In life you must try and be the type of person that your dog thinks you are!"

This book celebrates the many unique and multifaceted roles that men play today. It's a collection of wise, funny, and sometimes tender thoughts, along with some good advice, by and about great guys. Enjoy sharing it with all the great guys in your life!

BARBARA MILO OHRBACH

All men are
poets at heart.

RALPH WALDO EMERSON

Combine a tough mind
and a tender heart.

MARTIN LUTHER KING, JR.

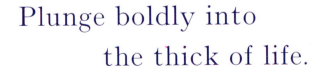

Plunge boldly into
the thick of life.

GOETHE

To this day I cannot see a
bright daffodil, a proud gladiola,
or a smooth eggplant without thinking of
Papa. Like his plants and trees, I grew
up as a part of his garden.
LEO BUSCAGLIA

I watched a small man with thick calluses
on both hands work fifteen and sixteen
hours a day. I saw him once literally bleed
from the bottoms of his feet, a man who
came here uneducated, alone, unable to speak
the language, who taught me all I needed
to know about faith and hard work by
the simple eloquence of his example.
MARIO CUOMO

My dad . . . he'd try anything—carpentry,
electrical wiring, plumbing, roofing.
From watching him, I learned a lesson
that still applies to my life today:
No matter how difficult a task may seem,
if you're not afraid to try it . . . you can do it.
And when you're done, it will leak.
DAVE BARRY

I guess the only thing that's important is
that he *was* my father. He was some guy,
my Dad was. Some guy.
JACK LEMMON

By profession I am a soldier and take
pride in that fact. But I am prouder—
infinitely prouder—to be a father.
DOUGLAS MACARTHUR

It's passionately interesting to me that
the things I learned in a small town,
in a very modest home, are just the things
that I believe have won the election . . .
I owe almost everything to my father.
MARGARET THATCHER

I want to thank

the good Lord

for making me a

Yankee.

JOE DIMAGGIO

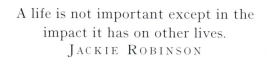

A life is not important except in the impact it has on other lives.
JACKIE ROBINSON

It ain't braggin' if you can do it.
DIZZY DEAN

Just keep going. Everybody gets better if they keep at it.
TED WILLIAMS

People look at me and get the feeling that if a guy in a wheelchair can have such a good time, they can't be too bad off after all.
ROY CAMPANELLA

Think to yourself,
"I'm going to hit the ball," and you can.
TY COBB

Inspire children.
HANK AARON

Age is a question of mind over matter.
If you don't mind, it doesn't matter.
SATCHEL PAIGE

Winning has a joy and discreet purity to it that
cannot be replaced by anything else.
A. BARTLETT GIAMATTI

Never let the fear of striking out
get in your way.
BABE RUTH

The more I practice

the luckier
I get.

ARNOLD PALMER

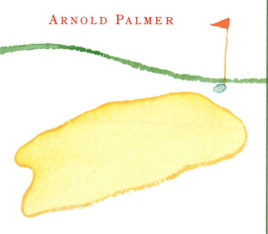

If you are caught on a golf course during
a storm and are afraid of lightning, hold up
a 1-iron. Not even God can hit a 1-iron.
LEE TREVINO

Golf is a game the aim of which
is to hit a small ball into an even
smaller hole with weapons singularly
ill-designed for the purpose.
WINSTON CHURCHILL

Take pleasure not in the score,
but in the game.
BOBBY JONES

I've known the agony and the ecstasy.
I'm convinced I've got more of
both ahead of me.
GREG NORMAN

There's a perfect shot out there
trying to find each and every one of us.
All we got to do is get ourselves
out of its way and let it choose us.
THE LEGEND OF BAGGER VANCE

Basically what my father has taught
me is that if you come from truth
everything will be okay.
TIGER WOODS

To a young boy,

the father is a

giant

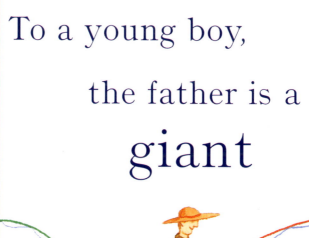

from whose

shoulders

you can see

forever.

PERRY GARFINKEL

Mothers all want their sons to grow up to be president, but they don't want them to become politicians in the process.
JOHN F. KENNEDY

He may be president, but he still comes home and swipes my socks.
JOSEPH P. KENNEDY, ON HIS SON JOHN

Every son, at one point or another, defies his father, fights him, departs from him, only to return to him— if he is lucky—closer and more secure than before.
LEONARD BERNSTEIN

How did I know he was going to become Leonard Bernstein? You know, every genius had a handicap. Beethoven was deaf. Chopin had tuberculosis. Well, some day I suppose the books will say, "Lenny Bernstein had a father."
SAM BERNSTEIN, REMEMBERING HIS OPPOSITION TO HIS SON'S MUSIC CAREER

It's only when you grow up, and step
back from him, or leave him for your own
career and your own home—it's only then
that you can measure his greatness and
fully appreciate it. Pride reinforces love.

MARGARET TRUMAN

As long as I have been in the White House,
I can't help waking at 5 A.M. and hearing the
old man at the foot of the stairs calling and
telling me to get out and milk the cows.

HARRY S TRUMAN

Nothing in life is more liberating than
to fight for a cause larger than yourself,
something that encompasses you but is
not defined by your existence alone.

JOHN McCAIN III

Son, there is no greater thing than to die
for the principles—for the country and the
principles that you believe in.

JOHN McCAIN JR.

Make yourself
necessary to

someone.

R A L P H W A L D O E M E R S O N

Life is what happens to you while
you're busy making other plans.
JOHN LENNON

If you have to ask what jazz is,
you'll never know.
LOUIS ARMSTRONG

Even if you're on the right track,
you'll get run over if you just sit there.
WILL ROGERS

Talent must not be wasted. . . .
Those who have talent must hug it,
embrace it, nurture it, and share it, lest
it be taken away as fast as it was loaned
to them. Trust me. I've been there.
FRANK SINATRA

I'm one of these guys—I love what I do,
so I never work a day in my life.
TONY BENNETT

When I painted houses, I'd paint any color
you wanted. But now I'm playing music,
and I do it my way.
BRUCE SPRINGSTEEN

Well done

is better than

well said.

BENJAMIN FRANKLIN

It is often easier to fight for one's
principles than to live up to them.
ADLAI STEVENSON

Just be what you are and speak from your
guts and heart—it's all a man has.
HUBERT HUMPHREY

The grandest of these ideals is an
unfolding American promise:
that everyone belongs, that everyone
deserves a chance, that no insignificant
person was ever born.
GEORGE W. BUSH

I have opinions of my own—
strong opinions—
but I don't always agree with them.
GEORGE BUSH

We must use time wisely and forever realize
that the time is always ripe to do right.
NELSON MANDELA

Leadership is a combination of strategy
and character. If you must be without one,
be without the strategy.
NORMAN SCHWARTZKOPF

Leadership is the art of getting someone
else to do something you want done
because he wants to do it.
DWIGHT D. EISENHOWER

If you would be loved,
love and be lovable.
BENJAMIN FRANKLIN

Winning isn't everything,

but wanting
to win is.

Vince Lombardi

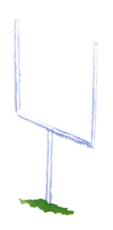

One loss is good for the soul.
Too many losses is not good for the coach.
KNUTE ROCKNE

There are no traffic jams along
the extra mile.
ROGER STAUBACH

"Wait'll next year!" is the favorite cry of
baseball fans, football fans, and gardeners.
ROBERT ORBEN

I learned much more from defeat than
I ever learned from winning.
GRANTLAND RICE

Have you called your momma today?
I sure wish I could call mine.
BEAR BRYANT

Success is being able to come home,
lay your head on the pillow and
sleep in peace.
HERSCHEL WALKER

I don't know
what you
could say
about a day

in which you
have seen
four beautiful
sunsets.

JOHN GLENN

There are only two lasting bequests
we can hope to give our children.
One of these is roots; the other, wings.
HODDING CARTER

I loved those years of being
Mr. Mom. One of the saddest days
in my life was when Jennifer said,
"Dad, I can wash my own hair."
BILLY CRYSTAL

The night you were born I ceased being my
father's boy and became my son's father.
That night I began a new life.
HENRY GREGOR FELSON

You don't raise heroes, you raise sons.
And if you treat them like sons,
they'll turn out to be heroes,
even if it's just in your own eyes.
WALTER SCHIRRA SR.

I can do one of two things.
I can be president of the United States
or I can control Alice.
I cannot possibly do both.
THEODORE ROOSEVELT

One word of command from me is
obeyed by millions . . . but I cannot
get my three daughters . . . to come
down to breakfast on time.
VISCOUNT ARCHIBALD WAVELL

It is admirable for a man to take his
son fishing, but there is a special place
in heaven for the father who takes
his daughter shopping.
JOHN SINOR

Sit loosely
in the

saddle
of life.

ROBERT LOUIS STEVENSON

There were times when my pants
were so thin that I could sit on a dime and
tell if it were heads or tails.
SPENCER TRACY

The guy who invented the first wheel
was an idiot. The guy who invented
the other three, he was a genius.
SID CAESAR

It takes twenty years to make
an overnight success.
EDDIE CANTOR

Horse sense is what a horse has that
keeps him from betting on people.
W. C. FIELDS

When you're younger, you want to be
sure that by the time you're
eighty years old you can sit on the
bench and look back and say,
"Man, I did it all. I didn't miss a thing."
BILL COSBY

Tomorrow comes to us at midnight very clean.
It's perfect when it arrives and it puts itself
in our hands and hopes we've learnt
something from yesterday.
JOHN WAYNE

Heart is what separates

the good
from the great.

MICHAEL JORDAN

Expect things of yourself.
MICHAEL JORDAN

If I were given a change of life,
I'd like to see how it would be to
live as a mere six-footer.
WILT CHAMBERLAIN

Becoming number one is easier than
remaining number one.
BILL BRADLEY

Excellence is the gradual result of
always striving to do better.
PAT RILEY

To be a great champion,
believe you're the best.
If you're not, pretend you are.
MUHAMMAD ALI

I don't like money, actually,
but it quiets the nerves.
JOE LOUIS

To be a champion, you have to believe in
yourself when nobody else will.
SUGAR RAY ROBINSON

I think sleeping was my problem in school.
If school had started at 4:00 in the afternoon,
I'd be a college graduate today.
GEORGE FOREMAN

Everybody

needs a hug.

It changes your metabolism.

LEO BUSCAGLIA

Show me a good loser and
I'll show you a loser.
JIMMY CARTER

There is nothing I love
as much as a good fight.
FRANKLIN DELANO ROOSEVELT

Be the very best you can be.
Let nothing deter you; let nothing
stand in your way, and go for it.
COLIN L. POWELL

One man with courage
is a majority.
ANDREW JACKSON

Ask not what your country
can do for you—
ask what you can do
for your country.
JOHN F. KENNEDY

Do something.
Either lead, follow,
or get out of the way.
TED TURNER

New York is still here.
RUDOLPH GIULIANI

Let your tongue
speak

what your heart
thinks.

DAVY CROCKETT

Every shot not taken is a goal not scored.
WAYNE GRETZKY

I've had a good relationship with police all
over the world. I've been stopped,
and we've always come to terms.
MARIO ANDRETTI

Sometimes, you have to lose before
you can learn how to win.
DALE EARNHARDT

Citation was the most intelligent
horse I ever rode. It's a crime to take
the money for riding such a horse. . . .
It's a privilege and honor.
EDDIE ARCARO

Everybody must learn to lose
because you can't play the game
if you can't take losing.
ARTHUR ASHE

There is nothing—absolutely nothing—
half so much worth doing as simply
messing around in boats.
KENNETH GRAHAME

Three things
in human life
are important:

The first is to be kind.

The second is to be kind.

The third is to be kind.

HENRY JAMES

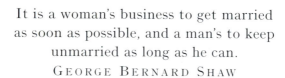

It is a woman's business to get married
as soon as possible, and a man's to keep
unmarried as long as he can.
GEORGE BERNARD SHAW

My most brilliant achievement
was my ability to be able to
persuade my wife to marry me.
WINSTON CHURCHILL

I kissed my first woman and smoked
my first cigarette on the same day.
I have never had time for tobacco since.
ARTURO TOSCANINI

When women go wrong,
men go right after them.
MAE WEST

When a man sits with a pretty girl for an
hour, it seems like a minute. But let him
sit on a hot stove for a minute—
and it's longer than any hour.
That's relativity.
ALBERT EINSTEIN

If a man yells in the woods and
no woman hears him, is he still wrong?
ANONYMOUS

If you are ever in doubt as to
whether or not you should kiss a pretty girl,
always give her the benefit of the doubt.
THOMAS CARLYLE

A man loves his sweetheart the most,
his wife the best, but his mother the longest.
IRISH PROVERB

The game isn't over until it's over.
YOGI BERRA

Laughter is wine for the soul—laughter
soft or loud and deep, tinged through with
seriousness. . . . The hilarious declaration
made by man that life is worth living.
SEAN O'CASEY

The lives of truest heroism are
those in which there are no great deeds
to look back upon. It is the little things
well done that go to make up a
successful and truly good life.
THEODORE ROOSEVELT